Where Was God
When I Needed Him Most?

Mother's Promise Led Me to Christ

David R. Clark

A sequel to the bestselling book,
Where Was God When I Needed Him Most?: Finding Christ Even in My Darkest Hour

Where Was God When I Needed Him Most?: Mother's Promise Led Me to Christ

Cover background photo by Sara Clark

Edited and typeset by Jeannie Culbertson

Proofread by Elizabeth Tripp

ISBN: 979-8-9875005-3-8 (ebook)

ISBN: 979-8-9875005-4-5 (paperback)

*The author can be contacted by email at authordavidclark3@gmail.com.

Dedication Page

This book is dedicated to both my mom and dad, who reared me to live a Christ-centered life, putting my faith and hope in Jesus Christ.

Download the *Free Gift*

READ THIS FIRST

Thank you for going on this journey with me. To show my appreciation to you for buying this book, I'm offering to you, as a **FREE** gift—a .pdf document consisting of sample (1) scripture journal pages and (2) log pages for keeping up with providing positive reinforcement to others.

Download at the following link or QR code:

https://author-david-r-clark.ck.page/a8042e7107

Table of Contents

Prologue

Mom's situation was dire. It was obvious very early in her pregnancy with me in 1972 that this was no ordinary pregnancy. She was hospitalized during the first trimester and remained hospitalized mostly for the remainder of the pregnancy. The culprit of her health difficulties stemmed from the way the uterus was situated—she was losing circulation in her left leg, causing her significant harm.

As the pregnancy progressed, the doctor, being gravely troubled over her life-threatening condition, tried, unsuccessfully, to convince my mother to abort me. Notwithstanding her repeated refusals to proceed with an abortion, the doctor was so convinced she needed to abort me that he attempted to abort me without her knowledge or consent.

The doctor's efforts were thwarted when my dad became aware of the circumstances. I was born healthy and strong in every way in January 1973. Mom recovered from the health complications she experienced during the pregnancy.

Mom had a pivotal experience during the pregnancy even amidst the whirlwind around her and the torcherous pain that defined her existence. This was an experience that remained with Mom throughout her pregnancy and gave her strength to persevere, notwithstanding her pain and suffering and the chaos surrounding her doctor's efforts to abort me.

One Sunday afternoon, while she lay in her hospital bed, Mom was considering the unborn child—me—she then carried. In her mind's eye, she could see the man she hoped I would become. Even in this nightmare scenario, Mom described that, while she was thus pondering, a light filled her hospital room and this heavenly bliss overwhelmed her soul. During this moment of divinity, there was no pain, no threats to her health or her unborn baby's life, there was only joy.

It was during this life-changing moment when Mom promised me, her then-unborn baby, that she would never let me forget the love she knew I must have had for Jesus Christ. This book details a sampling of what Mom has done and continues to do to keep her promise to me. Come with me as I explore the powerful effect Mom has had and still has on my life.

INTRODUCTION

In my book, *Where Was God When I Needed Him Most?: Finding Christ Even in My Darkest Hour*,[1] I discussed my present circumstances of being bedridden for more than eight years (nearly nine years now) due to being exposed to toxins while serving in the United States Army as a Soldier in Iraq, how my life has completely changed having been turned totally upside down, the anguish I have experienced wondering why God let these things happen and whether He had abandoned me, to discovering that God did not and will not abandon me or anyone.

I further wrote about the rest Jesus offers in Matthew 11:28–30 ("Come unto me, all ye that labour and are heavy laden, and I will give you rest.Take my yoke upon you, and learn of me; for I am meek and lowly in heart: and ye shall find rest unto your souls. For my yoke is easy, and my burden is light." KJV). In our adversity and trials,

---

[1] The book, *Where Was God When I Needed Him Most?: Finding Christ Even in My Darkest Hour*, will be referred to as *My Darkest Hour* and this book, *Where Was God When I Needed Him Most?: Mother's Promise Led Me to Christ*, will be referred to as *Mother's Promise*, to plainly and easily distinguish the two books from the other.

if we turn to Him, Jesus will come to us and we will find peace in His presence that is overflowing and beyond description–a joy that fills the space where you are and envelops the soul, especially in the darkest hour.

In writing about this process of finding Jesus during my bedriddened state in *My Darkest Hour*, I wrote about experiences I had had with my mom while I was growing up that profoundly affected me and helped me find Christ as an invalid even though I had been feeling completely disconnected and abandoned by Him. One experience I included in the book was a story Mom shared with me about when she needed God's help when she and a friend were stranded on a raft in the ocean. Some of the other stories in *My Darkest Hour* involving Mom included being rescued from multiple tornadoes and overcoming hearing, speech, and learning obstacles.

Additionally, I wrote about how Mom was intent on surrounding us children with pictures, books, and other media that would establish a Christ-centered home wherein we could learn of Jesus. Both my mom and dad were anxious to share experiences they had wherein their respective faith in God increased. They explained how these experiences helped them grow to know Him more. In this environment, there were opportunities to exercise my own faith and, as such, build my own testimony.

During the editing process of *My Darkest Hour*, more than one person commented on the deep-seated impact Mom had on me. They noted the remarkable job Mom had done in teaching me about Jesus Christ. One person, in particular, commented that she hoped she was having that kind of impact on her own children. With those comments, I decided to write this book about my mom and the far-reaching effect her efforts to keep her promise to me during her pregnancy had had on my life.

In reviewing what I included previously in the book, *My Darkest Hour*, I realized it was only a portion of what Mom had done for me to teach me about Jesus. So, I decided to take some time now to go into more detail about my mom and her influence on me as a Christian. Some of what I write in this book will include portions directly from the book, *My Darkest Hour*, but this book will expand and elaborate on what Mom means to me, relative to my relationship with Jesus Christ.

Mom taught me who Jesus is so I could understand intellectually. Then, she showed me who Jesus is in my heart, so I didn't just know *about* Him, but I would *know* Him. She showed me through her own experiences the power of the name of Jesus and afforded me the opportunity to have my own experiences so I would know for myself the power Jesus can have in my own life.

This book is divided into three primary sections. The first section describes my mom, the kind of person she was and is, and how she kept her promise. This section comprises events *not shared* previously in *My Darkest Hour*, except there is a portion in section one about my mom's pregnancy in chapter one because it was during this pregnancy that Mom made her promise to me, her then unborn son, that she would never let me forget the love she knew I had for Jesus. It was this promise and Mom's effort to keep this promise that lays the foundation for the entire book.

The second section consists of experiences that were shared in *My Darkest Hour*. These experiences are critical building blocks to how Mom kept her promise and, as such, are repeated in this book, though with significant additional information in many places. I divided these experiences with my mom into two sections to clarify what was shared previously from the new material in this book.

The third section consists of seminal portions of the final chapters of *My Darkest Hour* to illustrate how Mom, keeping her promise never to let me forget the love I have for Jesus, helped me in my current adversity of being bedridden for nearly nine years.

[Author's note: While this book focuses primarily on efforts Mom made, my parents, both Mom and Dad, were a team in keeping Mom's promise not to ever let me forget about my love for Jesus.]

SECTION I

Mom's Love

Behold, children are a heritage from the Lord, the fruit of the womb a reward.

Psalm 127:3

This section contains mostly experiences previously not shared.

Chapter 1

The Promise

During my mother's pregnancy with me, she had serious health problems. While I did not reveal this in *My Darkest Hour*, her health problems were life-threatening. She spent most of her pregnancy in the hospital. As I grew up hearing my mother talk about her pregnancy, and the vast time she spent in the hospital, I believed that when a woman was pregnant, she went to the hospital and stayed there until the baby was born. Years later, I found out that ordinarily, a woman only goes to the hospital when she's ready to give birth.

In any case, my mother's health problems during pregnancy affected her left leg. She struggled to walk, partly due to an ulcer that developed on that leg, causing it to rot. Her doctor was very concerned about her health and her life. He spoke to her several times about having an abortion.

Besides his grave concerns for my mother's health, the doctor justified the idea of abortion by claiming I was underdeveloped. This notwithstanding, my mom remained vehemently opposed to abortion. After fervent prayer together, my parents discussed the matter and decided not to heed the doctor's advice. In answer to their prayers, the Lord impressed upon their hearts that Mom's health would be preserved and that I would be born healthy.

Still, people who knew my mom were also concerned about her health and tried to persuade her to at least consider an abortion. At one point, after many attempts to gain my mother's consent for an abortion, the doctor took matters into his own hands. He moved my mom from her hospital room near the other expecting mothers to a room in another wing of the hospital.

This unexpected move bothered my mom. She kept asking the nurses why she had been moved, but they would not respond. Then, when the nurses began preparing her for a medical procedure and would not explain what was happening, Mom became insistent about knowing what was going on. Still, they refused to answer her questions.

Mom continued asking questions and pleaded for understanding of what was happening. Finally, the doctor came in. He was very upset and noticeably frustrated. He told Mom that she was moved because he did not want the other expectant mothers to know there was a woman in the hospital who had to have an abortion. And she was going to have it whether she wanted it or not.

My mother was shocked. Those nurses and that doctor were preparing her for an abortion without her knowledge or consent.

My father entered the hospital room right when the doctor was yelling at my mom. Dad asked what was going on and why the doctor was so upset. The doctor explained the situation. My dad somehow kept his cool and calmed the doctor down.

Dad asked the doctor to perform some additional tests and then, depending on the test results, reconsider the idea of an abortion. Before he received the results, the doctor continued trying to persuade my mom to abort me. He told her that if I were born, I would be deformed and have other health problems.

When the test results were given to the doctor, he came back to speak with my parents. He was bewildered because the tests, for the first time, came back normal. From that point on, he made no more efforts to abort me.

Mom's health was preserved, and I was born in January 1973 with no medical issues or defects, just as the Lord promised in answer to my parents' prayers. Mom says that I was born healthy and strong in every way. I even weighed over eight pounds.

I am grateful that God answered my parents' prayers and eased their concerns. I am also grateful my parents were firm in opposing my abortion and withstanding the doctor's arguments and pressure. Without God's intervention, *I would not be here.*

As a parent now, I cannot imagine the anxiety Mom must have been experiencing. First, she spent months in the hospital. The longest I can remember spending hospitalized is about ten days. Life in an extended-hospital stay is challenging in many ways. I simply cannot envision being in the hospital for months.

Dad was in pilot training with the United States Air Force. He did all he could to care for both his wife in the hospital and two babies at home, a three-year-old son, Brian, and a two-year-old daughter, Lisa, but he was limited. So, Mom had to rely on others greatly during this timeframe.

Eventually, Dad's command found out the extent of his situation. In my mom's words, a superior officer in Dad's command asked him, "You mean to tell me that, after flying these jets, you don't know when you land whether your wife is alive or dead!?" So from that point forward, Dad's primary duty mission was to take care of his wife and children.

Beyond the extended hospital stay, Mom's circumstances were exacerbated because she had the two babies at home, who each needed their momma. Being in the hospital and enduring this arduous pregnancy, Mom could not provide the care Brian and Lisa needed.

In trying to grasp how helpless Mom must have felt, I cannot fathom the internal struggle she battled with her competing maternal instincts for her unborn child, which necessitated her extended hospital stay, versus her two babies at home, who needed her to be there for them. Life would have become much simpler to follow the doctor's prodding toward an abortion. In so doing, Mom's life-threatening health issues would be resolved, and her two babies at home would have their mother back.

Nonetheless, with what must have felt like the weight of the world on her, Mom had a pivotal experience during the pregnancy even amidst the whirlwind around her and the torcherous pain that defined her existence. This was an experience that remained with Mom throughout her pregnancy and gave her strength to persevere, notwithstanding her pain and suffering and the chaos surrounding her doctor's efforts to abort me.

One Sunday afternoon, while she lay in her hospital bed, Mom was considering the unborn child—me—she then carried. In her mind's eye, she could see the man she hoped I would become. Even in this nightmare scenario, Mom described that, while she was thus pondering, a light filled her hospital room and this heavenly bliss overwhelmed her soul. During this moment of divinity, there was no pain, no threats to her health or her unborn baby's life, there was only joy.

It was during this life-changing moment when Mom promised me, her then-unborn baby, that she would never let me forget the love she knew I must have had for Jesus Christ. This experience fueled Mom's drive to persevere through any and all such adversity.

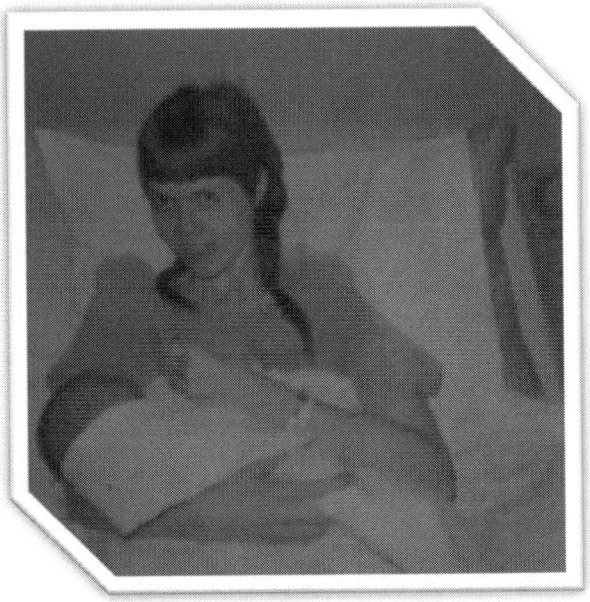

Mom holding me in the hospital shortly after my birth.

I have previously asked my parents why they were so strong. Mom told me repeatedly that she relied on her faith in the Lord and the promptings of the Holy Ghost that the baby she carried was healthy, strong, and normal in every way; and that, upon my birth, her health would return, and she would be fine. Having made this promise to me, she was willing to endure it all to keep her promise.

And his mother treasured up all these things in her heart.

Luke 2:51

Chapter 2

Motherhood

My very first memory of my mother: I was in my crib looking up at her and thinking how lucky I was to have the mother I had. To me, she was the most beautiful person on earth. Don't ask me to explain how I remember that; it's just something that has stayed with me. I knew at a very young age that my mother was somebody special.

She grew up with much faith in Jesus Christ. She knew the importance of prayer even from a very young age. In *My Darkest Hour*, I shared my mom's raft experience when she was a very young girl living in Okinawa while her father, Henry Griffith, was stationed there in the 1950s (this story is also found in Section II below). This experience stands out because it taught me, even as a very young boy, the reality of God, prayer, and faith in Christ; that God knows the worries even little children have and that He will answer their prayers, too!

There are many other stories my mom would share with us about her growing up years. She was such a good story-teller that even my friends would come by and we would listen to her share her stories for hours. The Holy Ghost was always present in great measure when Mom shared her experiences. Some of my friends had never felt God's love in such abundance before meeting my Mom. While I cannot do her stories justice, I will attempt to share a sampling of them here.

[*As a sidenote, Mom is writing a book in which she will share many of her experiences*.]

Mom's faith in Jesus Christ and godly love for others continued throughout her childhood and adolescence. My Grandparents Griffith (Mom's parents) had eight children. One child died shortly after birth. Being the second oldest living child, Mom made it her mission to do things that needed to be done before her parents could even notice that it needed to be done.

Grandma Griffith would often gleefully say, when she found something done before she could get to it, "Oh, it looks like my little brownie has been here." (In folklore, a brownie was a friendly spirit who did household chores when no one was looking.) Mom never wanted her parents to know that she was the person who had done the chore. My Grandpa Griffith, while reminiscing decades later about my mom, would say, "Whenever I think of Jan, I always picture her with a dishcloth in her hand because she was always cleaning something or other."

In 1957, when Mom was ten years old, her mother, Grandma Griffith, gave birth to twins, Brenda and Barbara. To be helpful, my mom stepped in as a "second mom" to the twins, providing much of the mothering for them. The twins were babies number six and seven. Grandma's health was not very good, particularly at that time. So, Mom's help with the twins was needed and appreciated.

When Mom was 12 or 13, during a visit to her aunt's house in Nashville, Tennessee, she took her then 3-year-old twin sisters out for a walk. Two men in a laundry truck approached Mom and asked her to come over to the truck. Being extremely naïve, Mom walked over to the truck as requested.

When she was close enough, one man leaned down through the truck door window and kissed my mom, as she tells the story, "*Right on my mouth!*" Being such a young, naïve girl, Mom was stunned not knowing why this stranger had done this. At this point and before anything further could happen, Mom heard the voice of the Lord urgently admonish her, "Grab your sisters' hands and *RUN!"*

From a young age, Mom knew the voice of the Lord and was always quick to obey. On this occasion, Mom's lifetime of faithfulness put her in a position to hear and understand the Lord's voice, especially in a moment of extreme danger.

When she was 17 or 18, Mom was a front-seat passenger when the car she was in was hit by another car in an automobile collision, which happened when the driver was making a left-hand turn at a traffic intersection. In those days, there were no seat belts in cars. So, as a result of the collision and no seat belt, Mom's body was thrusted forward violently causing her head to go through the windshield, then she bounced back into her car seat.

Mom's first inclination was to ensure that her friend, who had been driving, was okay—although Mom's injuries were far worse. When Mom reached out to her friend, her friend noticed a lot of blood and panicked because she assumed it was her blood. Mom began to lift her head exposing a horrific head wound, Mom's friend then realized that the blood was not hers but was coming from Mom's severely injured head. With this realization, she screamed even louder and exclaimed, "*It's not my leg! The blood is coming from your head!!*"

Emergency personnel arrived on-scene of the automobile collision. After assessing the severity of the injuries, Mom, having suffered a significant head injury, was taken to the hospital by ambulance, where she underwent life-saving emergency surgery. Later that same night, after her surgery and as Mom was sleeping in her hospital bed, the nurses brought in another patient to take the other bed in the room. This other patient was whimpering due to the pain she was in.

The nurses did not know how to help Mom's new roommate, so they just left her to her tears. Wanting to help, Mom asked this other patient if it would be okay if she prayed with her. The other patient said, "Yes, please." Trying to understand the circumstances, Mom left her bed to help her roommate. Keep in mind, Mom was recovering from a serious surgery she had just undergone to save her life due to the blunt-force trauma she experienced when her head went through the car windshield in the car accident. Mom had no business getting out of bed.

If I had been in that situation, I likely would have been frustrated with the nurses for putting her in the bed beside me. The incessant whimpering couldn't have been easy for Mom to hear with the splitting headache she most certainly had. Mom's first inclination, however, was to reach out to this woman, offer compassion, and pray for her.

Mom crawled on her hands and knees to her roommate's bed. Mom said that her head felt so heavy; it just hung between her shoulders, making getting over to the other bed a very difficult task to accomplish. Her head was heavily wrapped in bandages from the surgery.

When Mom finally made it to where the other woman was in the room, Mom's appearance startled this weeping woman because of all the surgical dressing around Mom's head. While still on the floor, Mom grabbed the patient's hand and prayed with her. At the end of the prayer, the woman had calmed down, and she was able to sleep.

This is just a very small sampling of the person who would become my mother. I grew up listening to stories like these that instilled in me the importance of prayer, faith in Jesus Christ, and God's power to rescue.

Then they cried to the Lord in their trouble,
and he delivered them from their distress.

Psalm 107:19

CHAPTER 3

A Christ-Centered Home

I grew up in a home centered around Jesus Christ. I do not remember a time when Jesus was not the center of all we did. In the mornings, we had family prayer before we went to school, and in the evenings, before we went to bed, we also had family prayer. When we ate meals together as a family, we offered a blessing upon the food and thanked God for the food we ate. Mom and Dad encouraged us children to pray over meals while we were at school.

Mom always made sure pictures of Jesus were in our rooms and throughout the house. We read the scriptures together as a family. Additionally, we discussed what we were reading and how the scriptures we read applied to us.

A very helpful tool when studying the scriptures, including as a family, is to record

- important points read,
- thoughts received while reading the scriptures,

- questions that came to mind during the reading,
- how these scriptures relate to other scriptures, and
- how what was read can apply today.

These notes can be just a few jotted-down thoughts or as detailed as you might like.

Click here to receive a FREE five-day sample of what this scripture journal might look like:

https://author-david-r-clark.ck.page/a8042e7107

We went to church weekly on Sundays—much of the day on Sunday was devoted to church services. We also went to church on Wednesday evenings. In high school, I attended a morning scripture study class called "seminary," which started at 6:00 a.m. each day before school. I was excited to begin seminary when I started high school because Mom had been a seminary teacher when I was much younger, and it looked like an awesome experience!

My dad and mom, my brother, Brian (age 4), in front, my sister, Lisa (age 3), behind Brian, and my dad holding me.

When I was young, Mom was always involved in teaching or fully engaged in some other church capacity. One thing impressed upon me was how important it is to prepare well for any opportunity to serve the Lord in the church. In preparing to teach a lesson, Mom spent hours upon hours studying the assigned lesson, but also reading everything else on the matter she could find.

One year, Mom was asked to put together a 10- to 15-minute drama production for the youth to participate in to help them grow. Mom took this opportunity and ran with it. The first *Star Wars* movie had come out. Mom built the play based on the movie with these huge elaborate props another congregation member built. Mom never did anything halfway. If she was asked to do something, she always went the extra mile to ensure success.

The point I learned as a very young child was that nothing but our best would do, especially when it comes to doing something for the Lord. Flying by the seat of our pants will never suffice. So with that, the more we are willing to sacrifice in the Lord's service, the more He sanctifies our efforts, which begets miracles right before our eyes.

> *Now to him who is able to do immeasurably more than all we ask or imagine, according to his power that is at work within us, to him be glory in the church and in Christ Jesus throughout all generations, for ever and ever! Amen.*
>
> **Ephesians 3:20–21**

Chapter 4

Spiritual Experience

During a trip to see Grandma and Grandpa Griffith in Kentucky, I had a special experience that remains with me. I was young; I just cannot remember how old I was. But, it was after a different visit—the time when I got lost in the field (as told in *My Darkest Hour* and in Section II of this book).

When we visited our grandparents in Kentucky, the adults and my older siblings would get together and play *Rook*, a card game. I was far too young to play. I always felt left out because it looked like they were having so much fun.

They were so competitive, especially Grandpa! Their verbal exchanges were comical to hear. But still, I felt left out, especially because I always had to go to bed while Brian and Lisa were able to stay up to play cards with the adults.

On one of these occasions, Mom came over to me where I was supposed to be going to sleep on the couch and kept me company while the others played. I asked her to share with me more of her spiritual experiences regarding God.

She and I spoke for hours. When the others were done playing cards, Mom kissed me goodnight and went to bed.

While Mom and I talked, I felt something peaceful, calming, and exhilarating inside. I did not have the words or the knowledge then to identify what I was feeling as coming from the Holy Spirit, but that is exactly what was happening. When everyone went to bed, I remained awake. I could not sleep. I got up out of bed and paced around near the couch where I was supposed to be sleeping.

Hours passed, yet for me, it seemed as though time stood still. I can remember the moment like it was yesterday; it left an indelible impression on my soul. Although a boy, in that moment, I wasn't seeing things with the immaturity of a boy, but with the maturity of the eternal spirit my body houses.

In this moment, I understood how brief, in terms of eternity, this life is. I did not see God, but I spoke with Him, as if I were personally before Him, and with the familiarity any son has with his father. I determined I would follow Jesus throughout this life and accomplish the purposes for which I was born. This hinge-point moment would not have happened if Mom had not taken the time to share her experiences and testimony of Jesus Christ with me earlier that evening.

> *While we look not at the things which are seen, but at the things which are not seen: for the things which are seen are temporal; but the things which are not seen are eternal.*

2 Corinthians 4:18

CHAPTER 5

Bless This Child

Mom is the definition of a "go-getter." If she sees something that needs to be done, she dives in and gets it done. Mom frequently puts others' needs and wants over her own, no matter how much the cost is to her.

A prime example of this is illustrated when Mom got out of bed in the hospital shortly after major surgery to save her life after the automobile collision, so that she could comfort and pray for the woman in the hospital bed next to her. There are many other examples.

During one of the many medical appointments Mom took me to in her efforts to help with my hearing (as told in *My Darkest Hour* and Section II below), she noticed a young mother crying in the hall. Mom can't stand to see anyone crying and do nothing to comfort that person. So she approached the distraught woman to find out what was happening. The woman told my mom that she had just found out that her very young child had cancer.

Filled with compassion, Mom embraced this woman whom she had just met to comfort her. It was as if they had been lifelong friends. Looking at this distraught woman in her tear-filled eyes, Mom asked her if she had faith in Jesus Christ and that He could heal her young child.

The woman affirmed that she did have such faith. Next, Mom asked this grieving mother if she would be willing to let elders from her church come and offer a blessing of healing upon her child. This woman readily agreed.

My dad was and is an elder in the church. He and another elder went to the hospital. In Jesus's name and by His authority, they blessed this young child to be made whole, healed of the cancer. By the grace of the Healer Himself, even Jesus Christ, the child was, indeed healed, and the cancer was gone.

This miraculous healing started with my mom. She could not stand seeing another mother crying. Seeing a need, Mom did not assume someone else would comfort this distraught mother. Instead, Mom took action herself to provide comfort, and ultimately, the Lord's healing.

So many times, when we hear of someone in need, we often say or think something like this, "Ah, that's too bad. Someone should do something to help. I would be willing to contribute to such a cause." Mom is not like that. If Mom ever hears about a family in need, she does all she can to organize an effort to help that family.

Another example took place in Alabama when I was fourteen years old. I don't even know how Mom found out about this family. But, when she became aware there was a family in need, with five or six children from my age and younger, Mom got on the phone immediately to gather donations. Mom then went to stores in town, met with the managers of those stores, and persuaded them to donate hundreds of dollars of food and other supplies the family needed. The final thing this family needed was an oven. Mom called around until she found a business willing to donate one.

Comforting a grieving mom in the hospital and organizing a drive to get a family what they desperately needed—in both instances, Mom did not even know them—are just two examples of Mom stepping up to help. There are countless examples of her doing similar things for many others, most often, anonymously. This is just how she lives her life. Treating people as such is how I imagine Jesus would be. Without trying to teach me anything, Mom's actions taught me volumes about Jesus.

Therefore, whatever you want men to do to you, do also to them, for this is the Law and the Prophets.

Matthew 7:12

CHAPTER 6

Dream Big

My mother is the type of person who dreams big and then sets out to achieve her dreams. Back in the 1970s, when I was just a boy, my mother became concerned about the incessant attacks on the family. Mom was and is not the kind of person who just sits there and blathers about how "they" should or should not do "this" or "that." So, my mom, a young mother with three small children, who only had a semester or two of college education beyond high school, and limited financial means, founded a national organization to defend the family called "Pro-Family Unity."

As president of Pro-Family Unity, Mom traveled all over the country advocating for the essentiality of the traditional family. People were attacking, as remains the case today, the traditional construct of a family with a man and a woman connected through the bonds of matrimony who, together, rear their biological children under one roof.

Some argued that women did not need their families, so they urged women to leave their husbands and abandon their children. Now certainly, there are exceptions to the traditional family model and some people have been able to establish happy family environments outside of this traditional format.

The point is, however, my mom saw something with which she disagreed, so she took action. Even with no college degree, having educated herself on the issues, Mom dreamed big in her aspirations to defend the family. She was just as comfortable amid United States Senators as she was playing with blocks with her young children at home.

Children's children are a crown to the aged,
and parents are the pride of their children.

Proverbs 17:6

CHAPTER 7

Unconditional Love

When Brian was in high school, he played on his school's varsity basketball team. At one point, the head varsity basketball coach, Coach Albano, felt his team needed a spark, so he approached my mom and asked her if she would come into the team locker room before the next game and speak to the players. She went in with a multi-page handout filled with inspirational stories and quotes from various people in and out of sports.

I remember seeing Brian and his team coming out of the locker room after that first time she spoke to them. The look on their faces was the look of the "eye of the tiger." The spark that had been missing was definitely there. Brian's team won that game handily by some 25 points. After that, Coach Albano had Mom come in to motivate the team before every game, both home and away, for the remaining two years Brian was in high school.

These young men responded favorably to the unconditional love Mom showed them, some of whom did not have that in their own homes. On Mom's birthday, as they left the locker room before the game started, each player had a flower, and each ran up to Mom where she was seated in the bleachers and gave her a kiss and a flower. By the end, she had quite a bouquet. The hundreds in the stands waiting for the game to begin stood by and cheered. Many of these young men turned their lives over to Christ and were baptized as a result of Mom's efforts with the team.

As a side note, Mom was ruthless in cheering for the team. She would often stand on the sidelines on the floor and cheer, even eclipsing the cheerleaders; well, her cheering eclipsed the hundreds of people who were there to watch the game. The school mascot was the Trojans. Everyone could hear her determined battle cry—*"Goooo Trojaaans!"* My heart beams with pride just thinking about it here today. Those boys on that basketball team knew that Mom loved them with everything in her and that she would either be the last to leave a sinking ship with them or be the wind to see them to victory. No matter what, she had their back!

During an away game, the opposing team's coach complained that Mom was disrupting the game with her cheering and her battle cry. The referee told Mom that only team coaches could be on the sidelines. Coach Albano quickly interjected that Mom was a coach for the team. So, she was allowed to remain on the sideline, and she cheered even louder!

I know she was doing this for my brother's team, but it taught me so much about striving to do the best you can in all you do. Mom knew nothing about motivating a group of high-school-aged young men. She loves her son. So, when asked to motivate the team, she dove in, completely devoting her heart and soul to the opportunity.

Each week, she went to the library, checked out several books, read those books, and then developed a ten to twelve page handout for these young men to read. In the way she loved these boys and believed in each of them, she taught them (and me) about Jesus.

There was one young man who was not keeping up with his academic studies and was about to be ineligible to play basketball. When Mom found out about this, she went to the respective teachers, developed a plan in which the young man could do extra credit in order to earn grades that would permit him to remain eligible to play. Mom was insistent that this young man be made to earn the grades; she was not asking for any unearned or special allowances.

Later, Coach Albano spoke with this young man and told him my mom believed in him and that he'd better not let her down. No one had ever believed in this young man before. What Mom did transcended basketball. For the first time in his life, this young man knew someone believed in him. He never had problems with his academic studies that could affect his eligibility to play after that.

In this instance, Mom did not sit down and talk to me about Jesus, but she taught me more about Jesus Christ than any words could have. This young man did not deserve another chance. The only thing he deserved was to be deemed ineligible to be on the team because he did not focus on his academic studies during the semester.

Nonetheless, someone—Mom—believed in him and extended an olive branch to him. Now, the parallel between what Jesus does for us and what Mom did for this young man is far from equivalent, but just as Mom gave this young man a second, undeserved opportunity and the chance to proceed forward, Jesus offers us an opportunity we do not deserve—salvation and eternal life.

> *For the grace of God has appeared, bringing salvation for all people, training us to renounce ungodliness and worldly passions, and to live self-controlled, upright, and godly lives in the present age, waiting for our blessed hope, the appearing of the glory of our great God and Savior Jesus Christ, who gave himself for us to redeem us from all lawlessness and to purify for himself a people for his own possession who are zealous for good works.*

Titus 2:11–14

CHAPTER 8

Share the Gospel

Hawaii

One year, I believe it was 1986, we were living in Hawaii at the time on an Air Force Base—what was then Wheeler Air Force Base. We were discussing as a family whom we would invite to the house for Thanksgiving dinner that year. Mom was intent on having someone come over with whom we could share the Gospel.

I remember I kept suggesting families with kids about my age, especially if they had daughters I wanted to get to know better. Mom's mind, however, was made up—it had to be someone with whom we could share the Gospel. She didn't wait for someone to just show up. Instead, Mom prayed, pleading with the Lord to direct her to someone who was ready for the Gospel.

Then, Mom went to work and asked anyone and everyone if they'd like to come to our house for Thanksgiving dinner—the repairman who came to fix the oven, the mailman, the airmen who checked military IDs at the base entry gates—she literally asked everyone! Unfortunately, those she asked already had plans.

The day before Thanksgiving, we still did not have anyone coming. Mom never lost hope. It was around 10:00 p.m. that evening when there was a knock at the door. We were surprised to open the door and see the missionaries because it was very late for them to be out and about. They brought a young airman, Larry Dennis, who was away from home for the first time on Thanksgiving.

The missionaries felt like they should bring Larry over to meet Mom, notwithstanding the lateness of the hour. The first thing Mom did was ask Larry whether he had any plans for Thanksgiving. He did not at the moment, so Mom invited Larry to our house for Thanksgiving dinner.

Larry came to our home the next day for dinner on Thanksgiving. We had a wonderful dinner. Larry was from Tennessee. Much of Mom's extended family lived in Tennessee. Mom spent much of her time growing up in Kentucky and spent many summer months with her cousins in Tennessee. With that connection, Larry felt right at home with us.

After dinner, we sat together in the living room, reading scripture and bearing testimony of Jesus. The moment the Lord's Spirit fell upon Larry was a special moment for each of us there. Larry came back to our house a few more times when he decided to follow the Lord, Jesus Christ, by entering the waters of baptism.

Mom did not need to include the entire family in this evangelical moment. In doing so, however, not only did the

Holy Spirit fall upon Larry, but the Spirit filled each of us present.

People can talk, but words fade with time. On the other hand, the Lord's Spirit, touches the soul in a way that cannot easily be forgotten. Mom had included me, and the rest of the family, in an experience beyond anything she could have provided otherwise, which transcended anything she could have said or done on her own.

Remember that it was when we were bearing testimony of Jesus that this divine manifestation of the Spirit occurred. When you share something of Jesus from the heart with someone else, the Spirit of the Lord fills the hearts of those present with indescribable peace and joy.

Unfortunately, folks all too often turn to illicit behavior to try to fill the hole in their hearts. *There is nothing that more abundantly fills and heals the holes in our hearts than does the Spirit of the Lord!*

This experience remained with me such that, as a father, before I became bedridden, I wanted my family to have the same experience. It was July 2013. We met together as a family and decided that we wanted to find someone who was prepared to hear and receive the gospel that very month and would be baptized.

As a family we prayed as we normally did, both morning and night, but in these prayers, we asked the Lord to direct us to someone who would be receptive to the Gospel of Jesus Christ and to following Jesus in being baptized. For me, as their father, it was a remarkable experience seeing my family join our faith together, united in an effort to share God's love with others and the blessing of baptism.

Like my mom, I didn't just wait for someone to pop up out of no where. I began asking everyone I could, but no one showed interest. It was getting late in the month and it began to look like we were not going to find anyone interested. We continued to pray and to have faith.

At the time, I was a youth minister in our congregation. A young man showed up at Church one Sunday wanting to learn more. We had him and his family over to our home for dinner on July 27, 2013. Having him in our house gave us the opportunity to share the Gospel with him and bear testimony of Jesus Christ to him.

He was baptized shortly afterward. I cannot think of many things that bring more peace and joy into one's life than to spread the Gospel. Regarding my family, I wanted them to see what happens when you exercise faith in the Lord. This moment with my family never would have happened but for my mom and her example in Hawaii.

Among others, there is another person we met while living in Hawaii with whom Mom and the rest of the family shared the gospel. His name is Rudy Dela Cruz; one of the kindest men you could ever meet. I mention him, not just because he is an amazing person, but because his situation was different than the others. Rudy was an atheist in 1983 when we first met him.

Rudy's wife, Anita, was pregnant when Mom first met her at church. Anita had been looking for someone to care for her son after he was born and after her maternity leave was up. Anita felt impressed to ask Mom if she would provide this daycare service for her son.

Rudy and Anita Dela Cruz

Mom had not been looking to become a home daycare provider. She, however, told Anita that she would watch her son, whom Rudy and Anita named, Andre. I was ten years old when Mom started watching Andre.

It was fun having a baby around the house. I remember one time when Mom ran out on a quick errand and left Andre at home. Andre soiled his diaper, and only Brian, who would have been 14, and me, 11 then, were home. Neither of us had had much, if any, experience changing diapers. We laid Andre down on a changing pad, then looked at the changing instructions on the back of the diaper packaging. Andre kept looking at us like, "Come on guys, even I know how this goes and I am just a baby…" In the end, we successfully changed the diaper!

Unlike the experience with Larry (and others), who was ready to receive Jesus in his life, Rudy was not. He was ordinarily the one who came by and picked Andre up in the evening. So, we had regular contact with him, though he was fairly reserved for the first two or three years. Mom did not try to pressure Rudy. She, however, continued to show him genuine Christ-like love. People are ready when they are ready. Trying to press the matter only creates problems.

After a few years, Rudy had a very close friend who died. Being an atheist, his friend's death was particularly difficult for Rudy. This tragedy caused Rudy to begin asking questions about God. Because Mom had let things go in the Lord's timing, and had not created tension by trying to force the matter on him, Rudy turned to Mom for answers.

It was not long before the Lord's Spirit fell upon Rudy and convinced him of the reality of God as well as the truthfulness of Jesus and His gospel. Brian baptized Rudy right before we moved from Hawaii to Alabama in 1987. Since his baptism 36 years ago, Rudy has been the epitome of a Christian.

Waiting on the Lord and His timing, while continuing to show an outpouring of Christ-like love, was a powerful demonstration to me that the Lord's timing and plan is always better than our own.

Alabama

In Alabama, and although her health limited her ability to leave the house and to go to church (more on this later in this section), Mom was always anxiously engaged in evangelizing. Working with the missionaries, there were many Sunday afternoons when 15 or 20 people would come to the house. Mom would often share her testimony of Jesus with us. Then everyone there would take turns bearing testimony as well.

The outpouring of His Spirit was so great that it was nearly palpable. I can remember feeling so "high" in the Holy Spirit that I still felt like I was walking on air even the next day at school.

Mom didn't just surround me with books and pictures of Jesus. She didn't just tell me stories about her experiences that brought her closer to Jesus. She didn't just ensure that I went to church. Mom did all of those things, but she also engaged me in experiences during and through which I was bathed in the glory of Jesus and, as such, became a convert myself.

Therefore, as God's chosen people, holy and dearly loved, clothe yourselves with compassion, kindness, humility, gentleness and patience.

Colossians 3:1

CHAPTER 9

Hard Lessons Learned

Mom spoiled me in a multitude of ways while I was growing up; after all, I was her baby! While it wasn't an everyday occurrence, it wasn't uncommon for me to come home from school to freshly baked cookies or a chocolate cake waiting.

Me as a baby.

A prime example of my mom spoiling me was my brother's and sister's birthdays. They were born 364 days apart, which meant that Lisa was born the day before Brian turned one-year-old. For many years, we celebrated their birthdays on the same day. Being the baby, Mom was always concerned that I would not understand why Brian and Lisa got presents while I did not.

So, Mom, for years, bought me a present for their birthday to make sure I didn't feel left out while they were opening their gifts. Truth is, I understood the circumstances long before she stopped giving me a present for their birthdays. But I wasn't going to turn down a present if Mom wanted to give me one!!

While Mom loved to spoil me, she never turned a blind eye to misbehavior. It was important to her that I not only have faith in the Lord, but that I show my love for Jesus by keeping His commandments ("If ye love me, keep my commandments" John 14:15 KJV). In that, honesty was very important to Mom.

There are a few incidences that illustrate this point. One such time came when I was probably four years old. Brian and Lisa were in school. Mom and I went to the store. While Mom was paying for her purchases, I saw a bin filled with individually wrapped Dubble Bubble gum. It was just there. I didn't see a price tag, so I grabbed three pieces.

I put one piece in my mouth. *It was so good*!! As we walked to the parking lot just outside the store, I proudly told my mom, "Hey, Mom, I got some gum. I have one piece for Brian. One piece for Lisa. *And my piece is in my mouth!*"

I was so proud of myself that I thought to get some gum for my brother and sister—I just knew that Mom was going to be so impressed with me! To my shock, Mom suddenly became very stern, asking me where I had gotten the gum. I responded, "Mom, it was over there by the cashier for anyone to take."

Mom grabbed my arm and took me to the store manager so I could confess my wrongdoing and make amends. The store manager got down on his knees so he was down at my eye level and he explained that what I did was stealing and that if I kept doing it, I would go to jail.

Instantly, the sense of pride I had been feeling of being considerate of my siblings left me and the fear of going to jail filled its void. Yikes! I don't know if Mom anticipated the response the store manager gave, but I definitely learned not to steal (which is part of being honest).

When I was around eight years old, a friend of mine had some matches. So, we decided to go and burn something. There was a hill not far from where we lived where we went and burned small sticks.

Doing this was incredibly foolish because the vegetation on the hill was very dry; one spark and that hill would have ignited in flames, leaving us stranded with no escape. When I got home, I went to the bathroom to change my clothes. It wasn't long before Mom knocked on the bathroom door, wanting to know what I had been doing.

Not realizing the strength of the smoke odor emanating from my clothes, I tried to skirt the question. Of course, the truth came out and Mom explained how dangerous playing with fire really was and the importance of being upfront about things.

Another incident happened one evening, when I was thirteen years old, and the electricity went out in our house. My parents lit candles so we could see. My brother was lighting napkins on fire from the candles. It looked like fun.

When he left, I decided to try doing the same thing. He made it look easy: "Get the napkin on fire just a little, then blow it out. Easy! What could go wrong?" I naively thought.

I lit the napkin on fire; then I started blowing. I learned the hard way that fire grows with oxygen! The more I blew, the bigger the flames became. I was right in front of the back door, so I tried to open the latch to the door to drop the fiery napkin on the ground outside instead of the carpet indoors.

With the napkin fully inflamed in my hand, I was having difficulty with the latch on the back door. Eventually, my hand involuntarily released the burning napkin. My eyes must have been as big as saucers as, in what seemed like slow motion, the fireball fell from my hand and landed on the carpeted floor indoors. I was so thankful when the inflamed napkin turned into ash when it hit the floor.

My hand was burned and was blistering up. I did not want my mom to find out, so I enlisted Lisa's help.

Obviously, it's pretty difficult to hide an injury like that. Mom was very upset when she discovered I had tried to hide my injury. I was grounded!

Unfortunately for me, during the time in which I was grounded, there was a big college basketball tournament coming to Honolulu, not far from where we were living at the time. My dad, Brian, and I had tickets to go to the tournament. We were so excited and anxiously awaiting going to watch some of the nation's best college basketball teams play.

Notwithstanding how excited we were about the tournament, Mom did not make any exceptions to my punishment, so I missed going. This was a hard lesson to learn, but I am thankful, looking back now, that Mom held her ground because it helped reinforce the lesson of honesty she taught me when I was much younger.

The final experience I am including in this book, wherein Mom taught me lessons in honesty, happened when I was sixteen years old. I remember the day clearly. I had come home from basketball practice and discovered a letter addressed to me from the auto insurance company, USAA. The letter was regarding "What to do in case of an accident."

Now, this story has many teaching points beyond just honesty—pride is definitely one of them. I say this because I remember thinking, *I don't need this. You've got to be an idiot to get into a car accident. All you need to do is be careful, practice "defensive driving" habits, and everything will be fine!* I did not utter this to anyone, but it is definitely what I was thinking.

You need to understand the context. I had just turned sixteen (the age in Alabama at which point a person can get a driver's license), and this was about a week after I had received my driver's license. So, with all of that driving "experience," unbeknownst to me at the time, I was too inexperienced to have come to such a supposition. A more experienced driver would never have come to such a wildly ignorant conclusion!

This was happening on a Wednesday, which meant we had church that evening. The youth were going on a hayride. This is where the honesty part starts to come into play. Before I left to go to church, Mom told me to come straight home as soon as the hayride was over.

I remember feeling so grown up being able to drive myself to the hayride. My dad had a small Dodge D-50 pickup truck he was letting me use. The most awesome thing about the truck was it had flame decals on the hood and down its sides. I thought I was pretty cool driving a truck with flames on it.

Dad's truck.

When the hayride was over, some adult leaders asked me if I could help transport the hay back to where it belonged. Instead of obeying my mom and going straight home, I lied and told the leaders that I was available to help. In my mind, I wasn't necessarily "*lying*" because I was trying to be of service and surely Mom would want me to serve. *I was rationalizing!*

My friend, John Reed, went with me to transport the hay. Everything went fine in dropping the hay off. But things came unhinged on the way home. There had been a light mist in the air that evening. It wasn't raining, but it was enough to cause the roads to be wet and slippery. Being inexperienced, notwithstanding my thoughts to the contrary, I did not understand the complexity of driving on slick roads.

Not long into our return trip after dropping off the hay, we were going down a hill toward a T-intersection. As I applied the brakes, the tires on the truck locked up, and, on the slick roads, the truck did not slow down. In my inexperience, the longer the truck slid, the harder I pushed on the brake pedal.

In my mind, I kept thinking that the truck was going to stop before the stop sign. When we continued to slide past the stop sign (thankfully, there were no vehicles in the intersection at the time), I kept thinking, *Surely the truck will stop before we go over the embankment on the other side of the T-intersection.*

Yet, when we flew over the embankment, I was thinking that everything would be fine as long as we stopped before hitting the trees in front of us. To no avail, we finally stopped when we hit the trees. Thankfully, we were both wearing seatbelts!

During this terrifying car ride, I was bouncing vertically up and down and John was bouncing horizontally to the front and then to the back of his seat. We were both shrieking in horror. We must have made quite the pair bouncing around that truck and hollering like little kids on a roller coaster ride.

When we finally stopped and made sure the other was okay, we decided to get out of the truck. My door opened just fine, but panick settled in again when John's door would not open. Later, we discovered that a tree root from an uprooted tree had pinned against the passanger door. Fortunately, outside of some bumps, bruises, and whiplash, we were both okay.

John and I walked about a half mile back to the house where we had just delivered the hay a few minutes earlier and where I called my parents. It was about 10:00 p.m. when I made the call. Dad came to where the truck was located in the trees. We finally got home at about 3:00 a.m. Mom was more interested in my well-being than disciplining me.

If I had been honest with my church leaders by telling them that my mom had told me I had to go straight home after the hayride (these were days long before cell phones, so calling my mom and asking for her permission was not possible), this automobile accident would never have happened.

While I did not understand it then, as a father now of six children, five of whom have driver's licenses, I now understand that Mom was trying to limit my exposure, being a very inexperienced driver, to complex driving circumstances in wet weather. All said, I am sure the Lord got a kick out of how I thought it was pure idiocy to get into an auto accident to me having an accident that very night!

While it might have been easier to let the behavior in each instance go unchecked, Mom chose to enforce standards of morality because she had not, she would have failed in her promise that she would never let me forget the love I had for Jesus Christ. While I was and am far from perfect, Mom was and is perfect in keeping her promise.

I know, my God, that you test the heart and are pleased with integrity. All these things I have given willingly and with honest intent. And now I have seen with joy how willingly your people who are here have given to you.

1 Chronicles 29:17

CHAPTER 10

Courage and Perseverance

Mom has experienced a great deal of health issues, especially since 1978. She suffers from a neuromuscular disease. Her mother also suffered to an extent as well as others in Mom's ancestry. While it is unknown, it is possible that my injuries suffered in Iraq from being exposed to toxins were exacerbated because of this hereditary disease.

In the 1980s and '90s, there were times when Mom was able to do more. Her work with Brian's high school basketball team in the 1980s is an example of her relatively brief periods of time when she had increased physical ability; however, Mom has been and remains homebound.

There have been many things Mom has missed out on. She is in her element when she is in the service of others—nothing brings her more joy in life than to help others find Jesus. The irony is, she has been significantly limited physically in doing this evangelical service she loves so much. I wrote *My Darkest Hour*; however, Mom can write volumes on that important topic describing how her adversity has brought her closer to God.

She has had many heart-wrenching moments suffering from debilitating health problems for 45 years. Nonetheless, she remains faithful to the Lord. She puts forth a happy face and lives life with courage and perseverance.

Considering my own disabilities that leave me bedridden as a result of my service in Iraq, I can think of no better way in which Mom could have kept her promise to her yet unborn son—me—that she would never let me forget the love I have for Jesus than to suffer physically herself and illustrate to me by the very way she lives her life that, in Jesus, we can find rest even amidst horrendous adversity.

> *The steadfast love of the LORD never ceases; his mercies never come to an end; they are new every morning; great is your faithfulness.*
>
> *"The LORD is my portion," says my soul, "therefore I will hope in him."*

Lamentations 3:22–24

SECTION II

Mom's Faith

Her children rise up and call her blessed; her husband also, and he praises her: "Many women have done excellently, but you surpass them all."

Proverbs 31:28–29

The following chapters are taken nearly verbatim from my book, My Darkest Hour, with some additional elaboration (significant in a few places). Each is a critical building block that helps describe how Mom kept her promise to me, which is why they are included here.

CHAPTER 11

The Power of Amazing Testimonies

When I was young, and as I mentioned before, my parents were very open in sharing their testimonies—their thoughts about Jesus Christ, not only bearing their testimony of Him, but sharing experiences in their lives that formed the foundation of why they believe that Jesus Christ is our Savior and Redeemer. They also shared the necessity of following Him, because He is the only way to our Heavenly Father's presence. One of my favorite things as a child was to sit and listen to my mother share her own experiences in the Gospel and share her testimony, stories, and spiritual experiences.

Mom had a lot of them, and she, as I said earlier, was an excellent storyteller. I would sit at her knee and listen to her share her experiences for hours upon hours. I often returned to ask her if she would please share more of her spiritual experiences with me.

Mom and me in the front yard of our house.

Her stories taught me about how real Jesus Christ is and how much He wants to be part of our lives. I learned that when we let Him in, Jesus can be an integral part of everything we do, and through the Holy Ghost, we can experience peace and joy, even when things are not going well. Listening to my mom taught me the importance of prayer and that God will answer those prayers when we have faith.

One of my mom's experiences stands out as I ponder her stories today because it taught me, even as a very young boy, the reality of God, prayer, and faith in Christ. As I alluded to earlier, when my mother was eight years old,[2] in the 1950s, her family lived in Okinawa. Her father, Henry Griffith, was in the Army and was there on assignment with the military.

At one point, there was a church activity at the beach. It was a potluck and a social. My mother and a friend got on an inflatable raft and went out into the ocean. They were having fun just floating on the waves. They did this independently, without permission, so no one knew where they were or what they were doing. Her parents, family, and church members continued enjoying themselves on the beach.

Before my mother knew it, they had drifted quite far from the beach. My mom said the people on the beach looked like ants because they were so far from the shore. They were just a couple of very young girls, and neither one could swim. Immediately, when they realized the danger of their situation, my mother offered a prayer asking God to protect them and help them to safety. As she finished her prayer, my mother had the distinct impression to paddle the water with her hand.

My mother did not know how to swim, and the idea of paddling was a new concept to her. But she had the impression of doing that, so she and her friend followed

---

[2] In *My Darkest Hour*, I mistakenly said that Mom was a few years younger.

God's prompting and began paddling. It wasn't easy, but they made it back to the shore.

Stories like this, and so many others, instilled in me the importance of prayer, faith, and God's power to rescue. Mom's stories about praying and receiving answers became personal to me at an early age.

Therefore I tell you, whatever you ask for in prayer, believe that you have received it, and it will be yours.

Mark 11:24

CHAPTER 12

God Hears a Young Boy's Prayers

When I was four, my dad was serving in the United States Air Force, and we lived in South Carolina. My mom's parents, Grandma and Grandpa Griffith, lived in Louisville, Kentucky. Grandpa was an avid gardener and homesteader. He loved going out, picking fresh berries, and making pies out of them.

He had a grape vineyard in his backyard and would make fresh grape juice. He also had fruit trees. I especially remember his apple tree. We had so much fun climbing the apple tree's branches and eating the apples right off the tree. I fell in love with apple pie by eating the pies Grandma made with the apples from that tree.

Grandpa's garden was filled with tomatoes, carrots, green beans, and the usual food you might find in a backyard garden. They lived in a typical neighborhood, so he was limited in how much he could grow, but he had access to some property where he could pick berries. There were raspberries and many others.

During one of our multiple visits from South Carolina to see Grandma and Grandpa Griffith in Kentucky, my grandpa and dad were going to that property to pick fresh berries. They invited me; I was so excited to be the only kid going with Grandpa and Dad to pick berries.

In my young mind, this property looked huge. It seemed like hundreds of acres with wide open fields, trees, and bushes. There were more berries than you could imagine. Each of us had a couple of baskets and was picking the wild berries. I loved these berries. We would pick them, wash them, put some sugar on top, and eat them. That was always a fun treat when we visited our Grandma and Grandpa Griffith.

In any case, I somehow got separated from my grandpa and dad. Again, I was a very young boy—around four years old. I was scared because I did not know where they were. I was all by myself in a place I had never been before. However, I knew where my grandpa had parked his big ole long red station wagon, a typical one that you would see in the 1960s and '70s.

I went to the station wagon, hoping to find one or both of them there. I got very worried when I couldn't see either of them at the car. After opening the door, I climbed into the backseat, not knowing what to do. I wondered what had happened to them and worried they might never come back.

As a young boy, growing up in a Christ-centered home and hearing stories of my mother drifting so far out to sea in Okinawa and praying and getting home to safety, I knew I needed to pray. I got down on the floorboard—I was small enough to do that with no problems. With as much faith as I could muster, I prayed my little four-year-old heart out to God that Grandpa and Dad were safe, that I would be safe, and they would find me soon. I pleaded with God that everything would be okay. When I finished saying that prayer, I got back up on the seat and looked out the car window. Grandpa and Dad were walking toward the car.

I do not think my grandpa or dad knew how scared I was. They did not seem even to wonder what had happened to me. But, that experience—I think it was my *first* experience—when I felt an overwhelming feeling of comfort as I prayed. Even at that young age, I knew God was telling me everything would be okay.

I am so thankful my mom shared her testimonies with me. This prompted me to have faith in the Lord as I prayed my heart out in the car. As a result, I learned I could pray, and God would hear and answer my prayers—providing comfort when I was afraid. This was no longer something my mom told me from her experiences, it was something I knew from my own experience.

> *Don't be afraid, for I am with you. Don't be discouraged, for I am your God. I will strengthen you and help you. I will hold you up with my victorious right hand.*

Isaiah 41:10

CHAPTER 13

Peace in the Storm

A few years after my experience in the berry field in Kentucky, and the subsequent experience I had after talking with Mom about spiritual experiences while the others played cards, I had another significant experience—a tornado scare—that reinforced my faith that God hears our prayers and answers them. In 1979, the Air Force transferred my dad from his Air Force assignment in South Carolina to a new assignment at an Air Force Base in Illinois.

Before getting into the details about the tornado, the move itself to Illinois was miraculous. These are details not shared in *My Darkest Hour*. Selling and buying homes in the late '70s and '80s was very difficult because mortgage interest rates were so high—in the double digits. Anecdotally, even in 1999 when Tara and I purchased our first house, any interest rate at 8% was considered to be good. Mortgage interest rates we've seen over the past 15 years or so—2% to 5%—have been exceptionally low.

My parents felt like the home in South Carolina would sell quicker if the house was empty. Trying to keep a house presentable to show to potential buyers at the drop of a hat with little children can be a challenge. So, my parents moved us out of the home in South Carolina; however, until the home sold, there was no place for us to go. Dad had to begin work at his new assignment, so he went on to Illinois. Mom and us kids stayed with Grandparents Griffith in Louisville, Kentucky, while we waited for the South Carolina house to sell.

After staying with Grandma and Grandpa for a while, Mom had the distinct impression that if she packed up and left with us kids the next morning, the South Carolina house would sell that very day. Going on nothing more than this prompting, Grandpa tried to persuade Mom to stay and see if the house, in fact, sold before heading out to Illinois. He had the obvious concern that if the house did not sell, then she would have had to make the trip back to Kentucky.

Under normal circumstances, Grandpa's reasoning made perfect sense—no need to expend the time and money for the trip to Illinois until the house actually sold. Mom felt like her packing up and taking us to Illinois when there was no indication that the house would sell was a show of faith. Indeed, the realtor called very, very late after we arrived in Illinois to let my parents know that the house in South Carolina had just sold.

Acts like this made an indelible impression upon me of the power of faith in Christ and the importance of always following the promptings from the Holy Ghost.

Seeing this inspired actions I describe in *My Darkest Hour* such as when my wife and I determined that we, putting our faith in Christ, would move to Utah from Alabama even if we had not found a place to live yet.

With the South Carolina house sold, my parents were able to move forward in purchasing a home in Illinois, which was in a little town near the Air Force Base where my dad worked. In those days, all the elementary-aged neighborhood kids would get together after school and play.

When snow covered the ground in the winter, we would build forts, have snowball fights, and have all sorts of fun. The *Star Wars* movie *Empire Strikes Back* was popular, so we pretended we were on the ice world fighting stormtroopers. We got together in the spring, summer, and fall as well.

There were dozens of us playing kickball, hide-and-go-seek, and other such games. The neighborhood was our playground. Many times, we played football and other games in our front yards. We had so much fun as neighborhood kids.

Nobody really worried about children's safety, and there was not much reason to be concerned. All the kids got along well, for the most part. I remember we would go outside in the morning. Our parents would not know where we were; they just knew we were in the neighborhood.

Then, when our parents needed us to come home, they would step out on the front porch and shout. When any of us would hear our mom or dad yelling our name, it was time to run home to have lunch or take care of whatever Mom or Dad needed. Afterward, we would go back out, find the other kids, and play more.

The summers there were very hot and humid. One summer, in June 1981 or '82, we had all gone outside and were playing kickball in the street in front of my house. We played for hours. It was exceptionally hot that day, so all the neighborhood kids decided to go to the community swimming pool, which was about a mile away.

I wanted to go swimming with all the other neighborhood kids on this particular day since it seemed like a cloudless, hot summer day. Off in the distance, however, there were two of the darkest black clouds I had ever seen. I paid little mind to them other than seeing they were there and being surprised by how dark they were.

I went inside to find Mom in her bedroom. I knocked on her bedroom door and told her that all the other kids were going swimming, and I wanted permission to go with them. In response, she said, "No, not today."

I was very unhappy with that answer. I wanted to go to the pool with my friends. I thought she was being unfair. I went to the living room and slumped onto the couch to watch TV. Shortly after I turned on the TV, a news flash announced a tornado warning. (But to be clear, I'm not sure if it was a tornado watch at that point or a tornado warning.)

I looked outside. The sweltering, cloudless, bright summer afternoon suddenly became very dark. The wind was blowing trash cans and other things down the street.

My dad called my mom. To this day, I still remember the phone ringing and my mom picking up.

Dad had seen on the news that a tornado was coming toward our general area, so he asked us to get to a safe place. In our house, a long closet in the inner center was our tornado shelter. My parents stored blankets, clothes, pillows, and stuff to cover ourselves from debris or anything that could injure us.

My brother, Brian, eleven or twelve years old at the time, was not worried about the tornado. He wanted to see it, so he did not want to get into the closet. Mom was with him, trying to coax him into our safe place. This whole time I was alone. I'm not sure where my older sister, Lisa, was, but I was in the closet.

My parents had always taught me to go to the Lord and He would be there, especially when I was frightened. With this tornado coming, I went to the Lord in prayer while in that closet and I prayed my little heart out. As I pleaded with God to save us, I had this comfort envelop me like a warm blanket.

I then knew everything would be okay. This feeling was so overwhelming that tears flowed from my eyes. I can't even imagine what would have happened if Mom had let me go to the pool. It was plainly divine intervention!

Looking back on this now, I see two times—once in that field in Kentucky and then in Illinois with this approaching tornado—when my soul was overcome with such overwhelming peace that I knew everything would be okay. This feeling was not self-generated, but rather an experience that entered my soul when my heart was in great turmoil. The contrast between being in great fear for one's life, compared to being filled with sweet love, peace, and joy, is beyond description. It can only be explained as an external, supreme force replacing fear with divine peace.

These experiences, also including the experience I had in Kentucky after the others went to bed when they finished playing cards, impacted me so profoundly that I am still talking about them four decades later. The loss in my life had I not had these defining moments is immeasurable! The credit goes to the Lord and His grace and mercy for giving me a mother who was keeping her promise.

After receiving the answer to my prayer for protection from the tornado, I got up and departed the closet to find my mom. I found her in the living room. I told her that everything was going to be okay. She said she knew that to be true.

It was still raining by this point, but it was a regular rain shower. You could see the sunlight coming through the clouds. Before long, the rain stopped, and everything was back to normal. Unbeknownst to me, when I was in the closet praying, a tornado came toward our house, but just before tearing into our neighborhood, the tornado dissipated into nothing.

> *Then they cried out to the LORD in their trouble, and he brought them out of their distress.*

He stilled the storm to a whisper; the waves of the sea were hushed.

Psalms 107:28–29

CHAPTER 14

The Lord Saves Us from the Storm

Pondering these events now, I can see my confidence in the Lord and His ability to rescue me continue to increase. This caused me to reflect on other times when I prayed and received His protection. For example, when I was nine, my brother played on the eighth-grade basketball team. They had a basketball game in December 1982 near New Baden, Illinois.

I remember that game well. My brother's team was fantastic; they were undefeated. In this game, however, Brian's team was losing by thirteen points at halftime. I remember seeing Brian when he came out of the locker room to start the second half. He had this look on his face of pure determination. Nothing would prevent him and his team from coming back and winning that game.

After a hard-fought second half, Brian's team did, in fact, come back to win the game. Brian had a large part in the comeback and ultimate win. His example and the efforts of his team taught me a lot about perseverance and resiliency. These lessons helped define me and have stuck with me even today, nearly forty years later. And yes, we were all very excited about the win.

My mother and I were the only ones from the family who went to the game—Dad was away on a trip, and Lisa stayed home. Mom and I went to the game with a married couple associated with the team, who were gracious enough to give us a ride.

As we walked through the parking lot to reach the car after the game, it began to get stormy. Once inside the car, the rain came down so violently that we could not see through the windshield, even with the wipers moving at top speed. We could not go anywhere for a while. The couple giving us a ride was in the front seat, the husband driving. Mom and I were sitting in the backseat, with her behind the husband and me behind his wife.

At the time, I was almost ten. Based on my previous experiences with prayer, I knew the Lord could protect us if we prayed to Him in faith. So, I suggested we say a prayer. From what I could see, the couple that had driven us were not exactly religious, but out of respect, they agreed.

My mother asked me to say the prayer. During the prayer, I asked for protection from the storm. After I finished, the rain let up enough so we could drive. While driving home, the man turned on the radio to track the storm. At one point, the radio host confirmed that a tornado was on the ground in New Baden, Illinois. The man driving the car said, "Oh, New Baden is right there," pointing to the town across a field to the right. On the left side, it was all forest. All you could see were trees.

At a certain point, we saw a path of destruction in the forest where trees had been blown over. The path continued across the highway, through the field to the town. It seemed very clear that if we had not stopped to pray, we likely would have been directly in the tornado's path or very close to it when it crossed that highway into New Baden.

By the time I was nine years old, the Lord had answered my pleas for rescue in very obvious and immediate ways. I am so thankful that Mom gave me the opportunity to say the prayer. As the adult, it might have been more obvious that she would offer the prayer instead of me, the nine-year-old.

> *Do not be anxious about anything, but in everything by prayer and supplication with thanksgiving let your requests be made known to God. And the peace of God, which surpasses all understanding, will guard your hearts and your minds in Christ Jesus.*

Philippians 4:6–7

Chapter 15

Faith and Determination

While many times, God answers our prayers quickly, Mom taught me it is important to maintain faith in Christ, even when God does not come to our rescue right away. One time for me related to my hearing. Another time was regarding my schooling.

Between the ages of one and five, I had a problem with fluid building up behind my eardrums to the point that I could not hear. During one of many medical appointments, the doctor told my mom that I could not hear seventy-five percent of what was happening around me. It had been that way since I was a little baby, though my parents did not know I was having problems hearing.

There were some clues, however. For example, I always wanted to turn the TV volume up really loud so I could hear the TV show. But, for everyone else, the volume was way too loud. Probably the biggest sign, though, was my speech.

When I was learning how to speak, my hearing was distorted. So, as a very young child just learning to enunciate his words, my speech was also distorted. I can remember as a young boy, in my mind, when I heard myself speak, it sounded like everybody else. I could not understand why people were having a hard time understanding me.

There were times when even my mom had trouble understanding me. Brian would come in and say, "Oh, he wants this," or "he wants that." So, Brian became an interpreter for me.

As I was about to enter kindergarten, Mom was growing ever more concerned with how I would do in a classroom setting, given my hearing and speech issues. She knew there had to be answers for my problems. She had taken me to various doctors for years in an effort to find out what could be done about my situation. Her efforts, however, had been unsuccessful.

As I was getting old enough to enter kindergarten, Mom's determination to figure out what could be done to help my hearing was unshakable. Ultimately, the decision was made to put tubes in both ears. In those days, it was an overnight inpatient surgical procedure.

Picture of me during kindergarten.

So, my parents dropped me off one night at the hospital. There were a bunch of us kids—probably ten or twelve of us—in the hospital room, getting ready for surgery in the morning. The next morning, we woke up, and my mom and dad were there at the hospital to show their support and their love.

Then, the nurses wheeled me off to the operating room. I remember they put a gas mask over my nose. I did not like the mask because of an odd smell—the gas—that I found to be horrid. I kept moving my head from side to side, trying to avoid the mask.

The next thing I knew, I was recovering, and the operation was over. I could not believe it because it seemed like I had been trying to avoid the gas mask just seconds beforehand. My parents were there after the surgery. They had bought all these toys to make my recovery go a little smoother. I thought I was the king of the world getting all those toys.

With those tubes in my ears and all the fluid drained from behind my eardrums, I could hear! That night, however, I heard things I had never heard before—like the air conditioning turning on, the house settling, and other noises you only hear at night when everyone is quiet and sleeping. For a five-year-old, who had never heard those sounds before, it was quite unsettling, to say the least! I just did not know what was happening. Being able to hear better opened a whole new world for me.

My speech, however, remained distorted. I remember hearing myself for the first time on an audio-recorded cassette tape. I was so embarrassed! I did not know that I sounded like that. My "j" sounds, "s" sounds, "th" sounds, and so many others were so badly enunciated that I could not stand to hear myself talk. To be frank, even as an adult, hearing my voice is always a jolt because I actually sound normal. In my mind, I still sound like I did when I was little.

In the first grade, I began attending speech therapy during school hours. Speech therapy in school continued from the first grade through the sixth grade. So, one day a week, the speech therapist pulled me out of class for our speech-therapy appointments. During these appointments, I would go and learn how to enunciate my letter sounds better and ultimately learn to speak better.

My first therapist would have me look at her tongue as she made exaggerated tongue movements to demonstrate what the tongue did in order to make those letter sounds. I am not sure how else she could have done it, but I never liked watching her tongue. On top of all this, my classmates knew why I was being pulled from class every week, which was very embarrassing for me!

Ultimately, the last sound I could not overcome was the “s” sound. I continued working with the speech therapists all the way into the sixth grade. Being twelve years old and being excused once a week from class to go to speech therapy to learn how to say the “s” sound was almost too much. Everybody knew where I was going and why I was going there.

After six years of regular speech therapy, I finally learned how to say the “s” sound properly. I felt like I had climbed Mount Everest! I recognized that this was a blessing from God and an answer to years of prayer. I was so happy and thankful that I no longer had to go to speech therapy. While this was an ongoing issue I dealt with throughout my elementary school years, and while it seemed, at the time, that I would never graduate from speech therapy, it was the faith in Christ Mom taught me to have that saw me through.

> *But this is why I was shown mercy, so that Christ Jesus could show his endless patience to me first of all. So I'm an example for those who are going to believe in him for eternal life.*
>
> **1 Timothy 1:16**

Chapter 16

Personal Values

Early on, in the first grade, the teachers could not understand me. Because of this, my learning was obstructed in many ways. I was quickly falling behind my fellow classmates. I was placed in the remedial, lowest classes. I will never forget walking into the bathroom and hearing the other students refer to me as "the retard." I really did not like being referred to that way.

In that context, I did not want to be in the slowest remedial classes. I did not need a participation trophy and kind words telling me I was special just as I was. I needed someone who would encourage me to be *better* than who I was. My mom and dad both did just that for me.

In some magnificent way, my mom and dad instilled in me the value of who I was then. They never made me feel like I was less, even being in remedial classes. At the same time, they encouraged and supported me in my efforts to challenge myself. Now that I am a parent, it amazes me how they could make me feel validated just as I was, yet support me in my efforts to better myself without diminishing the value I already held.

My mom and dad taught me to pray to the Lord when I am facing hard times. So, I prayed for God's help in school, including speech therapy. Nothing changed overnight. At the same time, I always felt God's love and knew He was there, supporting me through these difficulties. This also bolstered my self-esteem and gave me the courage to press forward.

As it was, I wanted to be with the smart kids like my brother. I remember my mom telling me that if I wanted to move up, I would have to work. Even when the other kids were playing outside, I spent hours every day reviewing my assignments. My mother tutored me because I had fallen so far behind in school. It took me a lot longer to get my homework done.

The motivation to improve in school came from me, but I wonder now what would have happened if I had not felt God's encouragement and if my mom had not supported me in this desire. What if my mom had told me to be content with where I was? What if she told me that I could not do it because I was not smart enough? What if she had not spent so much time with me daily? I thank God for a mother and father who supported me!

As I consider these events now, I see that these were formative years for me. I learned that while God answers prayers, sometimes His help is delayed in order to give me an opportunity to gain experience for myself; however, His support and encouragement can be felt throughout, even if it takes years for the hoped-for relief or rescue to be realized.

I remained in remedial classes throughout my first and second grades in elementary school. But, with the Lord's grace, my scholastic aspirations did not wane. During the third grade, teachers finally took notice of my improvement and advanced me from the remedial classes to what was called, at that time, the "average" classes. At the end of the third grade, and during a school assembly, I was recognized as the most improved student for the third grade.

I did not anticipate this recognition, but it motivated me to continue pressing forward. I was thankful to God that He was enabling me to improve as a student to be able to catch up with my fellow classmates. I had been so far behind. It was a relief to no longer be made fun of by other students for being so dumb.

I remained in the average classes in the fourth, fifth, and sixth grades. The desire to be in the advanced classes, however, was something that continued to weigh heavily on me.

In the seventh grade, the school put me in the same math course I had taken during a summer school math course. I believe I received an "A" in that summer school math class. But, if it wasn't an "A," it was no lower than a "B." I was very disappointed, so I went home and complained to my mom that I did not want to be in this lower class. I wanted to be in the advanced math class.

My mom, ever my defender, called the school counselor and told her I needed to be in the advanced math class. Mom and the school counselor went back and forth about why I should be advanced and why I should not. Ultimately, the school counselor said, "Mrs. Clark, which would you rather have? Would you rather have your son making A's and B's in the math class he is in right now, or would you rather have him make C's and D's in the advanced class?"

My mom's response is something that has stayed with me throughout the rest of my life. She told the school counselor, "You do not know my son; if you put him in the advanced class, he will make A's and B's, mark my words." And so they went ahead and put me in the advanced class, and I did make A's and B's, as my mother had foretold.

When I made it to the ninth grade to register for my classes, after struggling and persevering through elementary school, starting in the lowest most remedial classes, getting to the point of being in the average classes, and starting to get into the advanced classes in the seventh and eighth grade, I had been on a very long and difficult trek.

At one point, when I was five or six, my mom and dad began calling me "David the doer." I believed them! My mom's belief in me really helped counteract the negativity I experienced at school. I'm thankful that throughout my K-through 12th-grade years (and beyond), both Mom and Dad instilled a "can-do" attitude in me. Mom was insistent that I could do anything I set my mind to.

A child needs positive reinforcement from parents. In my experience, it is too easy to think positive things about each of my children and fail to convey those positive feelings to them. At the same time, criticism seems to always find its way out of my mouth and into my child's ears.

One thing I have done is pick a number of sincere compliments I want to tell each child each day. I have found this helpful when I have followed through on it.

As a free gift to you, I have put together a five-day challenge with sample log sheets you can use to record the sincere compliments you communicated to each child on the day the compliment was given. Set a number of compliments you are willing to give. It could be one or it could be ten; it depends on your particular circumstances.

Do this for five consecutive days. When completed, review your log to see what you communicated to your child during the five days. Of course, keeping a log is not required. It could be helpful, however, to be able to see on paper how and what you're actually doing.

The goal here is to become so accustomed to complimenting each child that it becomes a natural part of what you do without needing to set goals or keep logs.

Click here to receive the free five-day challenge with sample log sheets:

https://author-david-r-clark.ck.page/a8042e7107

We also glory in our sufferings, because we know that suffering produces perseverance; perseverance, character; and character, hope.

Romans 5:3–5

CHAPTER 17

Commanding the Storm

I also remember one particular Sunday in the spring of my senior year in high school. After attending church that morning, I was at home. I had finished my lunch and got up from the table to clean my dishes. I looked out the window and noticed the sky looking quite ominous. When you live in an area prone to tornadoes, you become familiar with a certain "feel" in the air and the look in the clouds as telltale signs of a severe storm with the potential for producing tornadoes.

With the sky darkening and that eerie feeling in the air, the wind started picking up. I could see from the kitchen window that some children from next door were playing on the neighborhood swing set. I suddenly felt that I needed to get those kids to their house.

I stopped washing my dish and bolted out the door. Those kids were small; both were younger than four years old. At the same time I reached those kids, their mother came running out of her house. The wind was picking up, and in a panic, she asked, "What's going on?"

I told her, "I don't know, but I think it's a tornado."

One of my high school senior pictures.

She grabbed her kids and hurried toward her house, the wind pushing her as she ran. I turned around, and sure enough, an enormous funnel cloud was bearing down on us. I then raced to my house. My mom was the only one at home. Frantically, I told her that a tornado was coming, and so we hurried to an inner closet in the house.

My mom, as she always did and had taught me to do, wanted to seek the Lord's help. Ordinarily, my mom would say the prayer in these circumstances, but she asked me to say it. The walls of the house were vibrating and shaking from the high winds, and I could hear the tornado approaching. Mom asked me to raise my hand to the heavens and command, in the name of Jesus Christ, that the storm dissipate and go away.

At that moment, I wished I still had the childlike faith I had when I was younger. It was hard because I *saw* what was coming. I saw the size of the tornado and could feel the house shaking. This monster funnel cloud was upon us, and my faith was weak.

I thought to myself in response to my mom's request, *"Well, you didn't see it!"* In my mind, at the time, I thought it was one thing to be in a closet as a young boy praying for safety from some danger I did not see than to see the immensity and power of this storm. I struggled to believe that a prayer from an eighteen-year-old nobody would stop this storm. Nonetheless, being obedient to my mother, I did as she instructed. In the name of Jesus Christ, I commanded that storm to dissipate right then and there, and, instead of causing damage, to provide rain for the farmers and gardens in the area.

As soon as I said my last word of that prayer, the house stopped shaking. The storm turned into a light rain that lasted an hour or so afterward. What once was a destructive storm became a rain shower providing water for the crops.

That was a tremendous experience for me because it was yet another example of God's power. I was humbled before the Lord to see His awesome power to control the elements. I was profoundly taught the power that comes by and through the name of Jesus Christ and the miracles that can happen therefrom. Mom could have prayed in the manner and with more faith than I had, but she deferred to me. This has been an anchor in my life, which would not have been so profound had Mom been the one who offered that prayer.

> *But as for you, continue in what you have learned and have become convinced of, because you know those from whom you learned it, and how from infancy you have known the Holy Scriptures, which are able to make you wise for salvation through faith in Christ Jesus.*
>
> **2 Timothy 3:14–15**

SECTION III

Mom's Wisdom

She opens her mouth with wisdom, and the teaching of kindness is on her tongue.

Proverbs 31:26

The following chapters are adapted excerpts from the book, My Darkest Hour. They are, in large part, the conclusions I draw in My Darkest Hour, with some adaptation. It's important to consider these points anew in this book because they help demonstrate how Mom's efforts to keep her promise to me before I was born have served to provide guidance and comfort to me these past nearly nine years.

CHAPTER 19

Where Was God?

I have been completely bedridden for nearly nine years due to injuries I sustained while serving as a United States Army officer in Iraq in 2007. Before I became bedridden, I was actively practicing law as an attorney, active in my church with multiple ministering responsibilities, and, most importantly, a husband and a father.

All of that changed when I became completely disabled and bedridden in 2014. I could no longer actively engage in the practice of law. I could no longer attend church for most of this time, which greatly limited my opportunities to minister (my church attendance and opportunities to minister to others brought me great joy). And my ability to be actively engaged with my wife and children was greatly hampered.

My body had finally succumbed to the physical ailments incurred from my time in Iraq. When I say that I became completely bedridden, I mean I could not sit up, get out of bed, or stand. My lungs struggled for breath, so

I required oxygen 24 hours a day. I was unable to speak above a whisper.

Yet, that wasn't the worst of it. My pain was intense—no, the word "intense" does not sufficiently convey the pain level. I endured excruciating pain in my arms, shoulders, hands, legs, and feet. It felt like every nerve ending in my body was on fire. And my muscles contracted, especially my hands, forcing my fingers to close into a fist. I could not do *anything* for myself. In 2018, my VA occupational therapist categorized me as suffering from quadriplegia due to neuromuscular disease, and prescribed treatment consistent with such.

It is now 2023, and thankfully, medications help prevent muscle contractions, but not completely. The prescriptions are positive, except my hands remain in a fist-like position. I have not been able to open my hands since about November 2014. I have limited use of my arms, cannot sit or stand, and remain on oxygen; the circumstances that led to my categorization as a quadriplegic due to neuromuscular disease remain. I only leave my bed to attend a few medical appointments each year.

It really puts everything into perspective when I take a moment to think about it. At any point of the day whether it was three, four, or even seven years ago, or looking forward two or three years in the future, whatever folks were or will be doing—whether it's a fun day at the pool or beach, a trip to the movies, or just sitting outside enjoying a pleasant evening watching the stars as they begin to appear in the sky, I have been and will be alone in my bed, isolated from all of it.

In these circumstances, and after many years, my isolation turned into a feeling of being abandoned by those around me, but by God as well. I often wondered where God was and where was His hiding place. Then, because of my mom's diligence in keeping her promise to me, I found Jesus again, only to realize that He had been there the entire time. The following chapters tell the story of how I found Christ Jesus again.

My Darkest Hour was written from the perspective of a composite moment I had one recent morning at 3:00 a.m. in which I wondered where God was. My thoughts turned to my various experiences growing up, many directly tied to my mom. As I considered these experiences, my mind settled on a research project I completed in 2018 regarding Jesus's yoke as recorded in Matthew.

> *Come unto me, all ye that labour and are heavy laden, and I will give you rest.Take my yoke upon you, and learn of me; for I am meek and lowly in heart: and ye shall find rest unto your souls. For my yoke is easy, and my burden is light.*

Matthew 11:28–30

CHAPTER 20

Christ's Indescribable Love

At this early morning hour, even after being pressed upon by my despair, I am encouraged by the Spirit I feel now as I think about these experiences wherein the Lord came to my rescue; these experiences I had because Mom would never let me forget the love I have for Jesus. My thoughts now turn to Jesus's "yoke" and research I had completed on the matter.

As noted, Jesus taught, "Come unto me, all ye that labour and are heavy laden, and I will give you rest. Take my yoke upon you, and learn of me; for I am meek and lowly in heart: and ye shall find rest unto your souls. For my yoke is easy, and my burden is light." (Matthew 11:28–30 KJV). I definitely felt that I was carrying a heavy load. It was a burden too heavy to bear. I needed Christ's rest.

In her book, *Hidden Wisdom and the Easy Yoke*, Celia Deutsch, a professor of Religion at Barnard College, wrote that Christ's central message in the yoke saying appears to be a beckoning to come unto Him and an invitation to take upon us His yoke and to learn of Him. It is "the invitation to discipleship."[3]

Deutsch further notes that the "rest" promised is the presence of Christ. This is so much more than a "break" from our burdens. It is the promise of His presence. So, to my question, "Where was God?" The answer is, in large part, He's there pleading with us to come to Him and receive the rest only He can offer, i.e., His presence.

The rest Jesus offers in verse 28 is different than the rest offered in verse 29. In verse 28, Jesus offers rest to all who labor and are heavy laden; He only asks that we come to Him. Deutsch notes the rest promised in verse 28 to all who come unto Jesus "is not a reward to be granted in the future. It is a gift for the present life…"

As such, the rest Jesus offers in verse 28 is from our burdens so that we might then, without the hindrance of those burdens, be able to take up His yoke—discipleship—and learn of Him. You see, the yoke is not a metaphor for an object we place around our necks, but rather, it symbolizes a new relationship we enter into with Christ through covenant—that of discipleship.

The "rest" promised in verse 29 is different. As the rest promised in verse 28 appears to be afforded to any who, in the present, come unto Christ, the "rest" promise in verse 29 appears to be some future eternal rest afforded to

---

[3] Celia Deutsch, *Hidden Wisdom and the Easy Yoke: Wisdom, Torah, and Discipleship in Matthew 11.25-30* (Sheffield England: JSOT, 1987).

those who indeed become His disciples becoming both meek and lowly in heart.

These principles touch my heart and teach me that as I turn and come unto Jesus Christ, I can have His presence. He would be with me and not off in some faraway part of the universe, unaware of me and the suffering I experience. As I thought about how much the Savior had blessed me, even in my darkest hours, I knew He had been with me. Further, by taking upon myself His yoke—discipleship—His rest would endure not only for now, but forevermore. Without the foundation my mom and dad set for me in Jesus Christ, this epiphany, which brought me such peace, would never have been realized.

To the Jews who had believed him, Jesus said, "If you hold to my teaching, you are really my disciples. Then you will know the truth, and the truth will set you free."

John 8:31–32

CHAPTER 21

Christ Took Upon Himself Our Burdens

The yoke saying further clarifies that, in addition to having taken upon Himself our sins, enabling us to find peace, Christ also took upon Himself all burdens we face in this life. The book of Isaiah describes the Lord as follows:

> *He is despised and rejected of men; a man of sorrows, and acquainted with grief ... he was despised, and we esteemed him not. Surely he hath borne our griefs, and carried our sorrows: yet we did esteem him stricken, smitten of God, and afflicted ... with his stripes we are healed. He was oppressed, and he was afflicted (Isaiah 53:3–7).*

Through Christ's atonement, Jesus took upon Himself not only the sins of the world, but also the pains, sorrows, and infirmities we experience. As we find relief from the weight of our sins through Christ because He has already suffered that burden for us, we can find relief in Christ from the weight of our pains, sorrows, and infirmities because He has likewise already suffered that burden for us.

David A. Bednar observed it is through the Lord's atonement that we can find rest. We take upon ourselves Christ's yoke and bind ourselves to the Lord through sacred ordinances and keeping the covenants associated therewith. He emphasizes the often overlooked and misunderstood principle that Jesus not only relieves us of, upon repentance, the burden of sin, but also life's travails and adversities. In his April 2014 General Conference talk, Elder Bednar taught the following:

> *Thus, the Savior has suffered not just for our sins and iniquities—but also for our physical pains and anguish, our weaknesses and shortcomings, our fears and frustrations, our disappointments and discouragement, our regrets and remorse, our despair and desperation, the injustices and inequities we experience, and the emotional distresses that beset us.*
>
> *There is no physical pain, no spiritual wound, no anguish of soul or heartache, no infirmity or weakness you or I ever confront in mortality that the Savior did not experience first. In a moment of weakness, we may cry out, "No one knows what it is like. No one understands." But the Son of God perfectly knows and understands, for He has felt and borne our individual burdens. And because of His infinite and eternal sacrifice ...*
>
> *He has perfect empathy and can extend to us His arm of mercy. He can reach out, touch, succor,*

heal, and strengthen us to be more than we could ever be and help us to do that which we could never do relying only upon our own power.[4]

It is one thing to know a gospel doctrine educationally, but it is quite another to know it through experience. I learned there is a God in heaven, and He has prepared a way for all these injustices to be made right—whether because of crimes of others (like school and other mass shootings or heinous crimes against women and children), mistakes we make, or acts of nature (illness, natural disasters, etc.). There is a loving God, and He mourns with us when these bad things happen. When we are in pain, He feels that pain with us.

The Creator of all things suffered for our pains and sorrows. He suffered for the sins of the world. He suffered the heartache, sorrows, and needless harm that is done in this world. People presume to claim that a loving God would not allow these things to happen. Yet, going through incredibly painful and debilitating experiences has taught me where God is when bad things happen—He is closer to us than any of us can really comprehend.

In the journal article, "The Yoke Is Easy, but What of Its Meaning?" published in the *Journal of Biblical Literature*, Matthew W. Mitchell asserts that translation of

---

[4] Bednar, David A. "Bear Up Their Burdens with Ease." The Church of Jesus Christ of Latter-day Saints. https://www.churchofjesuschrist.org/study/general-conference/2014/04/bear-up-their-burdens-with-ease.

the Greek word "χρηστός" as "easy" is a mistranslation and should read "good," "beneficial," or "useful."[5]

Using "good" instead of "easy" is in harmony with the certainty that there is nothing easy about discipleship (which is what Christ's yoke symbolizes), but it is good (useful and beneficial). The yoke saying takes on a dual meaning. First, in asking us to take upon us His yoke and find rest, Christ is inviting us to be free from our sins through His infinite atonement. Second, Christ's invitation is to all who have burdens of any kind to find rest or relief from such burdens in Him.

This is certainly the approach Alice Camille takes in the July 2002 edition of *U.S. Catholic.*[6] Camille says, "God remains with us in our suffering and burdens and wants to lighten our loads." I love this idea—this truth—that God remains with us in our suffering. *He does not abandon us*!

In this moment, and for years, I have been feeling heavy ladened. I feel the heavy weight of loneliness as it seemed the Lord and everybody else had forgotten me. To realize that Jesus's invitation to come to Him, learn of Him, and be one of His disciples applies to me brings me hope for my future. Even more, comprehending now that

---

[5] Matthew W. Mitchell, "The Yoke Is Easy, but What of Its Meaning?: A Methodological Reflection Masquerading as a Philological Discussion of Matthew 11:30," *Journal of Biblical Literature* 135, no. 2 (January 2016): pp. 321-340, https://doi.org/10.1353/jbl.2016.0017.

[6] Alice L. Camille, 2002. "Rest for the Weary." U.S. Catholic 67, no. 7 (2003): 43–45.

the physical pain and limitations and the spiritual and mental anguish I experienced, were some things the Lord took upon Himself, *my heart now soars!*

> *For we do not have a high priest who is unable to sympathize with our weaknesses, but one who in every respect has been tempted as we are, yet without sin. Let us then with confidence draw near to the throne of grace, that we may receive mercy and find grace to help in time of need.*
>
> **Hebrews 4:15–16**

CHAPTER 22

Conclusion

When I began writing *My Darkest Hour*, it was 3:00 a.m., and my life was bleak. Jesus assured His disciples, as recorded in John 16:33, "In this world, ye shall have tribulation: but be of good cheer; I have overcome the world." Why do we have to have tribulations in this life? In truth, this is a topic for a subsequent book. The essence, however, is that the Lord tries His disciples because He loves them and wants them to learn of Him (Psalms 119:71).

God has repeatedly and consistently come to my rescue. But, when I found myself bedridden, isolated, and in the darkest of places, I questioned where He was now. Although I wondered, at times, whether God had abandoned me, or whether I was no longer worth His time and attention, Mom's experiences and the experiences I had had *because* of what she taught me played in my mind, I came to realize that Jesus had not abandoned me at all! This brought me such peace and joy notwithstanding the fact that my physical, mental, and emotional circumstances had not changed one iota.

In researching what Jesus said in Matthew 11:28–30, regarding His rest and His yoke and then considering Isaiah 53:4 that Jesus bore our grief and carries our sorrow, I discovered the answer to my question of where He is when we need Him. The answer is found in two interconnecting folds.

1. Jesus took upon Himself not only our sins but also the suffering we experience from the burdens we carry in this mortal life. As such, Jesus alone is able to know exactly the burdens and suffering we experience. Having thus suffered for each of us, when you and I suffer, **Jesus is in the garden and on the cross suffering with us,** the very pain we presently experience. Jesus does not abandon us in our suffering—He suffers with us.
2. In these circumstances, **Jesus is there beckoning us to come to Him** and, when we do so, receive His presence—His rest—such that we might find relief during our adversity right now, and He invites us to take upon us His yoke, an invitation to discipleship, in order to have His presence with us forevermore.

Having taken our pain upon Himself in the garden and on the cross, Jesus prepared a way that we might find rest in Him in our suffering.

As I suffered, Jesus was there in the garden and on the cross, suffering with me what I was suffering! In coming to Him, and also in taking upon me His yoke (i.e., His burden—discipleship), Jesus is there with me, offering His rest, meaning His presence, which makes bearing the hardship become good, beneficial, and even useful.

Because of suffering, some use that to assert that there is no God, or that He does not care. Suffering, however, is part of this mortal life. I plan to discuss the reason for this in a subsequent book. These scriptures in Matthew 11 and Isaiah 53 affirmatively illustrate, however, that there is a God, and that He cares very much about our suffering. He took upon Himself all that you and I have suffered, are suffering, and will yet suffer.

This is not an uncaring God else He, God, would not have taken upon Himself our suffering. If we accept His invitation to come unto Him, find His rest, take upon us His yoke, the rest we find in our suffering becomes evidence of God and His love.

Intellectually, I knew most of these principles through scripture study, but then my life was taken from me, in a very real sense, where I was crippled and felt utterly alone, defeated, wondering whether I had done *anything* right in my life and whether it might have been better if the doctor had successfully aborted me to then finding Jesus *right there* in my pain. I now know the truth of Jesus in my very soul in ways I couldn't have before. I know that He has felt my pain and has overcome this very moment. Because I turn to Him, Jesus is with me offering peace and joy and to lead me through this trial.

As I conclude this book, I witness to you that Jesus Christ lives! I know that when I suffer, He suffers with me. When I turn to Him, taking His yoke upon me, I experience His rest in this life even amid tribulation, and I will receive eternal rest in the hereafter.

Jesus Christ has already taken upon Himself the burdens our hardships have caused. He has already suffered the pain and the sorrow. If we are willing to come unto Him and learn of Him, He is promising to replace our burdens, which weigh us down, with His, which can provide rest now and lift us up to His eternal rest, which is eternal life, forevermore.

Understanding that Jesus is in the garden and on the cross suffering with me, the exact heartache I am suffering, changes everything. He did not abandon me! He is intimately aware of me and my suffering. He is right there with me—closer than I ever could have imagined. Considering the totality of my present adversity, *I wonder where I would be right now if my mom had let me forget about Jesus.*

This is the impact moms and dads everywhere can have on their children. Parents have the blessing to share with their children that true peace and joy comes through the Prince of Peace—Jesus Christ.

This is done by affording children the opportunity to learn about Jesus, sharing personal thoughts and experiences about what Jesus means to the parent and how the parent finds peace and joy in Jesus, and allowing the child the opportunity to have such experiences for him or herself.

Many might question whether they have had any experiences worth sharing with their child. Please understand that these experiences don't have to be some grand event. What is important is to share with the child why the parent believes and has faith in Jesus Christ.

That's going to look different for everyone because we all experience life differently.

Some might be at the starting point of their own path to coming to learn about and to know Jesus. In that case, a parent should make the journey with his or her child. I can think of no better way help a child in this journey.

In this light, we are all growing and learning. Be open with your child about things you are presently learning and doing in your journey to Christ. My parents did this with me while I was growing up—they still do. This motivates me because I see the journey to Jesus Christ is a lifelong endeavor. In so doing, this is yet another way Mom is keeping her promise to me to never let me forget the love I have for Jesus.

Train up a child in the way he should go: and when he is old, he will not depart from it.

Proverbs 22:6

Epilogue

When I was sixteen years old, I had a dream quite different from most dreams I have had, if for no other reason than that I still remember it as if I had had the dream last night, though it was thirty-four years ago. In my dream, I was in front of the fireplace in my parents' house in their living room. My mother was sitting in a wooden rocking chair to the right side if you are looking at the fireplace.

I took a blank sheet of typing paper and wrote something on it. I did not remember what I wrote when I woke up from the dream, and I do not remember now, but I know what I wrote was about my mom. There were several reams of blank white typing paper stacked at least twelve inches high in the fireplace. There were no flames and no heat coming from the fireplace at that time. I placed the sheet of paper upon which I had written on top of the reams of blank typing paper.

After which, a single flame of fire ignited on top of the stack of paper. I remember being so surprised. I had not used a match or a lighter to ignite the flame, but there it was. In short order, the stack of paper was ablaze in a roaring fire that the fireplace could hardly contain.

As I stated, this dream was different than most other dreams I have had. It was so vivid. And it has become imprinted on my soul. I have wondered what, if anything, the dream might mean. One meaning seems evident: a mother keeping her promise to her child that she will never let him forget the love he has for Jesus creates a flame that can ignite a world in the truth of the Lord.

> *For you formed my inward parts; you knitted me together in my mother's womb. I praise you, for I am fearfully and wonderfully made. Wonderful are your works; my soul knows it very well.*
>
> **Psalm 139:13–14**

THANK YOU FOR READING

MOTHER'S PROMISE!

I really appreciate all of your feedback and I love hearing what you have to say.

I need your input to make the next version of this book and my future books better.

Please take two minutes now to leave a helpful review on Amazon, letting me know what you thought of the book.

Thanks so much!

—David

ACKNOWLEDGMENTS

I acknowledge my Lord and Savior, Jesus Christ. Without Him, there is no peace or joy. I thank Jesus for blessing me with a mom and dad who taught me about Jesus, giving me the proper foundation through which I can find this true peace and lasting joy even amidst trial and adversity.

I thank my editor, Jeannie Culbertson, for her indispensable work on this book. With *Where Was God When I Needed Him Most?: Finding Christ Even in My Darkest Hour* and now this book, Jeannie and I have been on an amazing journey together in Christ Jesus.

I also want to acknowledge my wife, Tara, and my children (Alexx, Richard, Jonathan, Sara, Megan, and Kirsten) for their love and support!

Do You Have an Experience to Tell?

Do you have an experience when God helped you through adversity? I would love to hear from you. I might use your story in another book. Please send me your story at authordavidclark3@gmail.com.

READ MORE

Steward Leadership: Jesus' Leadership Model

David published his first book on January 24, 2023, *Steward Leadership: Jesus' Leadership Model.* It can be found on Amazon in both paperback and ebook. Experts have called *Steward Leadership* "excellent," "thought-provoking," and "a unique look." The book has ranked high as a bestseller in the Amazon category of Christian Church Administration and has consistently been the #1 New Release in multiple Amazon categories for weeks after being published.

Where Was God When I Needed Him Most?: Finding Christ Even in My Darkest Hour

David published his second book, *Where Was God When I Needed Him Most?: Finding Christ Even in My Darkest Hour* on March 30, 2023. It can also be purchased on Amazon as an ebook and a paperback. Reviewers describe the book as "a must read," "highly recommended," "authentic and real," "deeply mov[ing]," a book that "should be in everyone's library," and a book that "truly brought me closer to God." The book has been ranked as the #1 bestseller in multiple Amazon categories including: Miracles and Spirituality; Inspirational Personal Testimonies; Spiritual Growth; Christian Leadership; Christian Missions and Missionary Work; and Disability Law. It has been ranked as the #1 New Release in several Amazon categories.

About the Author

David R. Clark received a bachelor of science degree from Auburn University at Montgomery in 1997. He graduated with a Juris Doctorate in 1999 from the University of Alabama.

Following law school, David served as an Assistant Attorney General for the state of Alabama, a Judge Advocate General (military lawyer) deploying twice in support of Operation Iraqi Freedom and Operation Enduring Freedom in the War on Terrorism, and a private attorney in Alabama.

David became 100 percent VA disabled in 2014 due to injuries suffered in Iraq. He has since earned a Ph.D. from Amridge University in Interdisciplinary Studies (leadership and biblical studies) in 2021 and a Master's degree in history from Liberty University in 2022. David is currently pursuing a Ph.D. in history at Liberty University.

Made in the USA
Columbia, SC
24 July 2023

20794138R00076